Sri Chaitanya
His Life & Precepts

BHAKTI
VINODE

LIBRARY

MANDALA
PUBLISHING

2240-B 4th Street

San Rafael, CA 94901

т. 415.460.6112

ꜰ. 415.460.5218

orders. 800.688.2218

ISBN: 1-886069-52-2

Designed and printed by

Palace Press International

Printed in China

Sri Chaitanya
HIS LIFE & PRECEPTS

BHAKTIVINODE THAKUR

MANDALA
PUBLISHING

Contents

Preface

Preface
Swami B.G. Narasingha

Bhaktivinode Thakur wrote over a hundred books, as well as numerous songs and articles, not only in his mother tongue, Bengali, but also in Sanskrit and English, to attract people everywhere to the sublime teachings of Sri Chaitanya.

At the end of the nineteenth century, the western world had risen to the height of power and influence. Its achievements in science, technology, and economic development seemed to know no limit. It had expanded its political power throughout the world, creating vast empires that dominated Asia and Africa, and with that came a sense of pride and conviction of the innate superiority of its civilization.

India was one of the conquered nations. Deemed backward, underdeveloped, poverty-stricken and bound by the superstitions of the past, it seemed to have little to offer its masters, the British, other than its natural resources and physical labor. What then could the people of this country possibly contribute to world civilization?

In 1896, an answer to that question arrived at Canada's McGill University in a brown package postmarked Calcutta, India. The package contained a small Sanskrit book, *Sri-Gauranga-Lila-Smaranam-Mangala-Stotram*, 104 verses summarizing the life and teachings of Sri Chaitanya Mahaprabhu. Accompanying this Sanskrit work was a 63 page booklet,

Sri Chaitanya Mahaprabhu: His Life and Precepts, which introduced the 16th century incarnation of Krishna to the English-
speaking world for the first time.

The author of both these works, Kedarnath Datta
Bhaktivinode Thakur (1838-1914), was a saint and scholar
in the Gaudiya Vaishnava tradition. Though himself a great
admirer of western thought and literature, he was confident
that once the intelligent people of the West came into contact
with Sri Chaitanya's teachings, they would recognize their
value and embrace them to their hearts' satisfaction. As
such, in this booklet he presented the quintessence of Sri
Chaitanya's life and teachings in such a simple and charming
way that even today, more than a hundred years later, people
throughout the Western world can still find great hope and
satisfaction from reading it.

The sum and substance of Sri Chaitanya's teachings is
"divine love," love for God, or Krishna. This philosophy of
love, wherein Krishna is the receiver and wholesale recipro-
cator of love with His devotee, is so charming and reassur-
ing that no unbiased person can resist it. Love is, after all,
the all-powerful force in the universe, and when it reaches
its perfection in love for God, all of mankind can rejoice in
peace and harmony. This was the gift of inconceivable value
and good fortune that Srila Bhaktivinode was sending to the
Western world.

A few years before he mailed his book to McGill University,
Srila Bhaktivinode had a vision in which he saw a great spiritual city rise up at Sri Chaitanya's birth site in Mayapur, near
the banks of the Ganges in West Bengal. In that vision, he saw
many thousands of people from both East and West, including
the world's most technologically advanced and wealthy coun-
tries, embracing the teachings of Sri Chaitanya. He saw the
realization of Sri Chaitanya's own prophecy, made nearly 400
years earlier, that his gift of divine love would spread to every
town and village in the world.

Inspired by this supernatural apparition, Bhaktivinode Thakur made it his life's mission to spread the teachings of Sri Chaitanya beyond India's borders. Sending a small book across the vast oceans to a people unaccustomed to India's spiritual traditions, though bold and courageous, was a small, even insignificant act. Now that we can see how a universal movement toward love of God is indeed taking shape, however, we can look back to this wonderful moment of deep faith and inspiration as its very beginning.

Knowing that the supreme good fortune of divine love was awaiting future generations, Srila Bhaktivinode wrote over a hundred books, as well as numerous songs and articles, not only in his mother tongue, Bengali, but also in Sanskrit and English, to attract people everywhere to the sublime teachings of Sri Chaitanya. The books and songs that flowed from his prolific pen came to form the basis of the revived Gaudiya Vaishnava movement whose practitioners can now be found in every country in the world.

It is our pleasure to once again publish Bhaktivinode Thakur's matchless gift to the world, *Sri Chaitanya: His Life and Precepts*. Those who are just on the threshold of discovering Sri Chaitanya's sublime teachings will derive great spiritual benefit from the present edition, while those already acquainted with them will delight in knowing that the vision and work of Srila Bhaktivinode Thakur are being carried on into the next millennium.

Introduction

Introduction

*The Vaishnavas die to live, and living try
to spread the Holy Name around!*

*Kedarnath Datta, who would later come to be
known as Bhaktivinode Thakur,* was born at Ula,
a very prosperous village in the Nadia district of
Bengal, on September 2, 1838 to an aristocratic
family who owned Govindapur (the present site of Fort
Williams in Calcutta). His childhood was spent in the home
of his maternal grandfather. At the age of fourteen he began
to study under one of the literary luminaries of the time,
Kashi Prasad Ghosh, the editor of the *Hindu Intelligencer.*
The paper was famous for its literary appeal, and the editor
attracted many writers eager to learn from him the correct
usage of the English language. Within a short time Kedarnath
was contributing articles to both the *Intelligencer* and the
Literary Gazette, another newspaper of the day. By the time he
was eighteen he had composed two books of an epic poem,
The Poriade, which he intended to complete in twelve vol-
umes. The first of these books can be found at the British
Museum in London.

During his stay with Kashi Prasad, Kedarnath became well
known for his great talent at debate and often exchanged ideas

on spiritual and literary subjects with eminent men of the day,
such as Devendranath Tagore and others, who found great
value in their discussions.

In 1860 Kedarnath published a pamphlet entitled *The
Maths of Orissa*, after visiting all the major *maths* (temples)
in the state of Orissa. In it he mentions a piece of land that
had been handed down to him from his ancestors: "I have
a small village, Chotimangalpur, in the country of Cuttack,
of which I am the proprietor. In that village is a religious
house, to which was granted, by my predecessors, a holding
of rent-free land. The head of the institution gave up entirely
entertaining such men as chanced to seek shelter on a rainy
night. This came to my notice; and I administered a severe
threat to the head of the house, warning him that his lands
would be cruelly resumed if, in the future, complaints of
inhospitality were brought to my knowledge."

Although Kedarnath began his life as a schoolteacher, by
1866 he had accepted a position with the government as a
Deputy Magistrate and was appointed Deputy Magistrate of
Dinajpur. It was in Dinajpur that Kedarnath first came in
contact with Vaishnavism, which had been prevalent under
the patronage of Raya Seheb Kamala Lochana. This great
Zamindar of Dinajpur was a descendant of Ramananda Vasu,
an ardent follower of Sri Chaitanya Mahaprabhu. Having
become acquainted with many of the Vaishnavas there,
Kedarnath secured copies of the *Chaitanya Charitamrta* and
a Bengali translation of the *Srimad Bhagavatam*.

After reading the *Chaitanya Charitamrta* for the first
time, Kedarnath formed a very high opinion of Sri Chaitanya
Mahaprabhu and thus began to regard Him as God. In association with the Vaishnavas of Dinajpur, he took to serious study
of Mahaprabhu's teachings. He made a comparative study of
Vaishnavism with reference to other religions by studying the
literature of Brahmoism, Christianity, and Islam, but found
the perfect consummation of his own thought in Vaishnavism.

Now Kedarnath became a full-fledged Vaishnava. He became so fixed in the principles found in the *Bhagavatam* that he delivered a powerful lecture on the subject in 1869, which attracted the attention of thousands and was later published as a small booklet, *The Bhagavat*.

Some years later, Kedarnath was transferred to a town called Champaran. There a *brahma-daitya* (a type of ghost) inhabited a great banyan tree while being worshiped by many degraded people. One day the father of a famous scholar came to Kedarnath for alms, at which time Kedarnath at once employed him in reading the *Bhagavatam* under the shade of the banyan tree which was inhabited by the ghost. After one month the *Bhagavatam* was completed, at which point the tree crashed to the ground, causing the ghost's permanent disappearance. Everyone was thankful for this act except a few dishonest persons who were worshiping the ghost.

After living in Champaran for only a few months, Kedarnath was transferred to Jagannath Puri accompanied by his family. He also brought with him his two favorite books—*Sri Chaitanya Charitamrta* and the *Srimad Bhagavatam*. He was happy to be posted at Puri where his object of worship, Sri Chaitanya, had lived for many years. The government commissioner was very pleased to have him in his division, and asked him to watch the affairs of the temple of Jagannath on behalf of the government. It was through Kedarnath's exertions that many malpractices were checked and the time for offering foods to the Deity was regulated to its extreme punctuality.

Kedarnath was especially entrusted to quell a rise against the government by a person named Bisikisena, who declared himself to be an incarnation of Maha-Vishnu. During the course of his investigation, Kedarnath found him to be a hoax and a culprit and charged him with transgressing government injunctions.

After his trial the fellow was sentenced to imprisonment

for a year and a half, but he died after a short time in jail. This man was possessed of unnatural powers, but as they were not the outcome of spiritual practices, he had to submit to Kedarnath. Bisikisena was held in dread by the common people. Everyone warned Kedarnath not to admonish him, even for the sake of justice, in view of the serious consequences that the yogi would inflict. Although Kedarnath was not a man of ostentation and did not generally allow people to know his true qualities and spiritual strength, he easily cut down the ungodly power of the impostor. With the fall of Bisikisena there arose a pretender named Balarama in another village, and there were also other so-called incarnations of God, but their plans were similarly frustrated.

Living in Jagannath Puri, Kedarnath's devotion to Sri Chaitanya Mahaprabhu grew very intense. He appointed a pandit named Gopinath to assist him in his study of the *Bhagavatam* with its commentary by Sridhar Swami. Hariharadas and Markandeya Mahapatra, who had studied *nyaya* (logic) and Vedanta in Nabadwip and Benares (two great centers of learning), began to study the *Bhagavatam* along with him.

Having learned Sanskrit grammar and literature under the great Isvara Chandra Vidyasagara, Dwijendranath Tagore, and others during his school days in Calcutta, Kedarnath continued to study the language. Many of the Vaishnava literatures such as the *Srimad Bhagavatam* were originally composed in Sanskrit text, and his knowledge of the language allowed him access to those great works. After finishing the *Bhagavatam*, he went on to study the works of Jiva Goswami and Rupa Goswami which he obtained from the library of the Raja of Puri.

Now he had mastered the philosophy of Vaishnavism and completed a book of his own in Sanskrit entitled *Datta Kaustubha*. He also began writing *Sri Krishna Samhita*, another book in Sanskrit, which later became famous. He wrote many other works during this period and began a class in which he taught the *Bhagavatam*. He stayed in Puri for five years, during which time all the Vaishnava leaders became impressed with his learning and devotion to the precepts of Sri Chaitanya Mahaprabhu.

From Puri he was transferred to different places in Bengal, and in 1878 he was stationed in Narail, in the District of Jessore. Here he became very popular as a Vaishnava Magistrate, and many kirtan groups would come to entertain him with their songs. From here he published *Sri Krishna Samhita* in 1889, and it soon received praise throughout India. Sir Reinhold Rest of the India Office in London expressed an opinion that seems to characterize the works of Kedarnath: "By presenting Krishna's character and His worship in a more sublime and transcendent light than has hitherto been the custom to regard Him in, you have rendered an essential service to your co-religionists."

While living in Narail, Kedarnath was initiated by Sri Bipin Vihari Goswami, and he adopted all the Vaishnava practices in their strictest form. He now resolved to interest the educated people in the principles of Gaudiya Vaishnavism as it was taught by Sri Chaitanya Mahaprabhu. With this in mind, he began publishing a Bengali monthly called *Sajjana Toshani (The Satisfaction of Pure Devotees)*, the first Vaishnava newspaper.

After staying for three years in Narail, he made a pilgrimage to various holy places. In Vrindavan he encountered a band of dacoits known as Kanjharas. These powerful bandits terrorized the roads surrounding the holy city, making it a practice to attack innocent pilgrims. Kedarnath brought this news to the government and after many months of struggle removed the bandits from Vrindavana forever.

From this time on, he preached extensively in large gatherings, explaining all the precepts of Chaitanya Mahaprabhu's sankirtan movement. In recognition of his vast learning

and devotion, the Goswamis of Vrindavan conferred upon
Kedarnath the title "Bhaktivinode."

It was also in Vrindavan that he met Srila Jagannath
das Babaji, the head of the Gaudiya Vaishnavas, who subse-
quently became the religious guide of Bhaktivinode Thakur
and helped him in his missionary activities. At this point
Bhaktivinode Thakur decided to take up the preaching of
Vaishnavism in earnest, and he founded a printing press
known as the Vaishnava Depository.

When he was commanded by his God in a dream to render
service to Sri Nabadwip Dham, the birthplace of Chaitanya
Mahaprabhu, Srila Bhaktivinode applied for a transfer to
Krishnanagar, which is a short distance away from Nabadwip.
In December of 1887 his transfer request was granted.

Srila Bhaktivinode was very happy to move to
Krishnanagar, having gone with the hope of discovering
the exact birth site of his beloved Deity, Sri Chaitanya
Mahaprabhu. While living in Puri he had acquired two books
that would help him in his archaeological investigation. One
of the books was the *Bhaktiratnakara* of Narahari Chakravarti,
and the other was a book authored by Paramananda Das.

One night, while on the roof of his residence in Nabadwip
during his deep meditation on the birthplace of Chaitanya
Mahaprabhu, he had a vision of a luminous building toward
the northeast.

The next morning he went to the vicinity of the place that
had appeared to him. During his investigation he came to
know of a place that was being adored by some of the local residents as the true birth site of Chaitanya Mahaprabhu. They
pointed out an extensive mound covered with Tulasi plants
and informed him that this was the actual site
of the house where Sri Chaitanya Mahaprabhu
had appeared. At last succeeding in his attempt,
he became extremely joyful. That same year
Srila Bhaktivinode composed and published his

famous *Navadwipa Dham Mahatmya* in glorification of every place within the circumference of Nabadwip.

In 1894 Bhaktivinode Thakur established Sri Nabadwip Dham Pracharini Sabha, with the ruling prince of Tripura as its president. The purpose of the Sabha was to arrange for the proper maintenance of the temple and worship of the Deities there. Srila Bhaktivinode Thakur was so devoted to this project that he was willing to go door to door himself, if necessary, to solicit contributions for the cause. *The Amrita Bazaar Patrika* noted the event with the following statement:

> *"Babu Kedarnath Dutt, the distinguished Deputy Magistrate, who has just retired from the service, is one of the most active members. Indeed, Babu Kedarnath Dutt has been deputed by the committee to raise subscription in Calcutta and elsewhere and is determined to go from house to house, if necessary, and beg a rupee from each Hindu gentleman for the noble purpose. If Babu Kedarnath Dutt, therefore, really sticks to his resolution of going round with a bag in hand, we hope no Hindu gentleman whose house may be honoured by the presence of such a devout bhakta as Babu Kedarnath will send him away without contributing his mite, however humble it may be."*

During his lifetime Srila Bhaktivinode Thakur wrote, edited, and published over 100 books in Sanskrit, Bengali, Hindi, Urdu, Persian, and English. Some of his more prominent works include: *The Maths of Orissa, The Bhagavat* (a speech), *Sri Krishna Samhita, Chaitanya Shikshamrita, Navadwip Dham Mahatmya, Sri Bhagavata Arka Marichimala,* and commentaries on the *Bhagavad Gita, Chaitanyopanishad, Ishopanishad,* and *Sri Chaitanya Charitamrta.*

Prior to the time of Srila Bhaktivinode Thakur, principles of Vaishnavism were unknown outside of India. In 1896, however, Bhaktivinode Thakur sent a copy of *Sri-Gauranga-Lila-Smarana-Mangala-Stotram* to the West, where it found its

way into the library of McGill University in Canada. During
the same years that Emerson and Thoreau were yearning
for Vedic wisdom, the *Journal of the Royal Asiatic Society* of
London (of which Bhaktivinode Thakur was a member) made
the following remarks:

"Under the title of *Sri-Gauranga-Lila-Smarana-Mangala-Stotram*, the well-known Vaishnava Sri Kedarnath
Bhaktivinode, M.R.A.S., has published a poem in Sanskrit on
the life and teachings of Chaitanya. It is accompanied by a
commentary, also in Sanskrit, in which the subject further
elucidated is preceded by an introduction of sixty-three pages
in English, *Sri Chaitanya Mahaprabhu: His Life and Precepts*,
in which the doctrines taught by Chaitanya are set out in some-
what full detail. This position, and more especially as against
Shankara and the
Advaita Vedan-
tists, is explain-
ed at length. The
little volume will
add to our knowl-
edge of this re-
markable reform-

In 1894, Bhaktivinode Thakur established Sri Nabadwip Dham Pracharini Sabha, with the ruling prince of Tripura as its president.

er, and we express our thanks to Bhaktivinode for giving it to
us in English and Sanskrit, rather than in Bengali, in which
language it must necessarily have remained a closed book to
European students of the religious life of India."

The work of preaching the Holy Name was also in
full swing, and it spread fast into the distant corners of
the globe. The *Sri-Gauranga-Lila-Smarana-Mangala-Stotram*,
with preface in English containing the life and precepts of Sri
Chaitanya, came out from Bhaktivinode's pen soon after the
discovery of Lord Chaitanya's birthplace and found its place
in all the learned institutions of both hemispheres.

The more the names of Lord Chaitanya and Lord
Krishna spread, the merrier Bhaktivinode Thakur became.

He thereafter made annotations of *Sri Brahma Samhita*, *Sri Krishna Karnamrta*, *Sri Hari Nama Cintamani*, and *Bhajana Rahasya*. He also edited, with commentary, *Srimad Bhagavatarka Marici Mala*, which contains all the most prominent *slokas* of the *Srimad Bhagavatam* pertaining to the Vaishnava philosophy.

Bhaktivinode Thakur's pen never tired, and it produced many other Vaishnava philosophical works. He would begin his writings very late at night, after completing his government work, and stay up until one or two o'clock in the morning composing songs and literatures. Most of his works appeared in the *Sajjana Toshani* magazine. He was equally engaged in writing and in preaching the Holy Name in many districts of Bengal. His personal appearances in villages had marvelous effects on the people. To maintain the center at Nadia he built a house at Sri Godruma dwip which is called Sri Svananda-sukhada-kunja. Here in this abode the preaching of the Holy Name continued in full swing.

In the beginning of the twentieth century he moved to live at Puri and built a house on the beachfront. Many honest souls sought his blessings and readily obtained them. Though he was leading the life of a renuniciate, he could not avoid the men of all description who constantly visited him. All of them received oceans of spiritual training, instructions and blessings. In 1910 he completely withdrew from the world and remained in a perfect state of samadhi, or full concentration on the eternal pastimes of the Lord. In 1914 he passed on to the blissful realm of Goloka on the day which is observed as the disappearance day of Sri Gadadhar.

A stanza written on the samadhi site of Haridas Thakur by Srila Bhaktivinode sometime in 1871 explains the influence a Vaishnava carries in this world, even after his departure:

He reasons ill who tells that Vaishnavas die
When thou art living still in sound!
The Vaishnavas die to live, and living try
to spread the holy name around!

Saragrahi Vaishnava

SRILA BHAKTIVINODE THAKUR'S
SARAGRAHI VAISHNAVA

In the year 1874 Srila Bhaktivinode Thakur published a philosophical book entitled *Datta Kaustubha*. During the same period of time he composed the following poem known as "Saragrahi Vaishnava":

Alas for those who spend their days
In festive mirth and joy:
The dazzling, deadly, liquid forms
Their hearts fore'er employ.

The shining bottles charm their eyes
And draw their heart's embrace;
The slaves of wine can never rise
From what we call disgrace.

Was man intended to be
A brute in work and heart?
Should man, the Lord of all around,
From common sense depart?

Man's glory is in common sense
Dictating us thy grace;
That man is made to live and love
The beauteous Heaven's embrace.

The flesh is not our own alas;
    The mortal frame a chain;
The soul confined for former wrongs
    Should try to rise again.

Why then this childish play in that
    Which cannot be our own;
Which falls within a hundred years
    As if a rose ablown.

Our life is but a rosy hue
    To go ere long to naught;
The soul alone would last fore'er
    With good or evil fraught.

How deep the thought of times to be!
    How grave the aspect looks!
And wrapt in awe become, Oh, I
    When reading Nature's books.

Man's life to him a problem dark
    A screen both left and right;
No soul hath come to tell us what
    Exists beyond our sight.

But then a voice, how deep and soft
    Within ourselves is left;
Man! Man! Thou art immortal soul!
    Thee Death can never melt.

For thee thy Sire on High has kept
   A store of bliss above,
To end of time, thou art Oh! His
   Who wants but purest love.

Oh Love! Thy power and spell benign
   Now melt my soul to God;
How can my earthly words describe
   That feeling soft and broad.

Enjoyment, sorrow, what but lots
   To which the flesh is heir;
The soul that sleeps alone concludes
   In them it hath a share.

And then, my friends, no more enjoy
   Nor weep for all below;
The women, wine, and flesh of beasts
   No love on thee bestow.

But thine to love thy brother man
   And give thyself to God,
And God doth know your wages fair
   This fact is true and broad.

Forget the past that sleeps and ne'er
   The future dream at all;
But act in times that are with thee
   And progress thee shall call.

But tell me not in reasoning cold,
    The soul is made alone
By earth's mechanic lifeless rules
    And to destruction prone.

My God who gave us life and all
    Alone the soul can kill,
Or give it all the joys above
    His promise to fulfill.

So push thy onward march, O soul.
    Against an evil deed
That stands with soldiers Hate and Lust
    A hero be indeed.

Maintain thy post in spirit world
    As firmly as you can;
Let never matter push thee down
    O stand heroic man!

O Saragrahi Vaishnava soul,
    Thou art an angel fair;
Lead, lead me on to Vridaban
    And spirit's power declare.

There rests my soul from matter free
    Upon my Lover's arms
Eternal peace and spirits love
    Are all my chanting charms.

—Bhaktivinode Thakur

His Life

The Life of
Sri Chaitanya Mahaprabhu

Hence, the life and precepts of Sri Chaitanya Mahaprabhu have scarcely passed beyond the boundaries of Bengal.

The object of this little book is to bring the holy life of Chaitanya Mahaprabhu and His precepts to the notice of the educated and religious people. Most of the books treating these subjects have hitherto been printed in the Bengali language. Hence, the life and precepts of Sri Chaitanya Mahaprabhu have scarcely passed beyond the boundaries of Bengal. A book has therefore been printed in Sanskrit type for circulation all over India. Our educated brethren of Europe and America have taken, of late, to the study of the Sanskrit language, and it is our belief that this booklet will go to their hands in a very short time. This book contains 104 verses with copious commentaries. It makes a succinct mention of all the anecdotes of the life of Sri Chaitanya Mahaprabhu as related in the famous book *Chaitanya Charitamrta* by Krishna das Kaviraj Goswami. Verses 75 to 86 inclusive will give an outline of the precepts of that great personage, Sri Chaitanya Mahaprabhu. With a view to help our English-speaking readers in going through the book, we have here summarized in English the contents of the work.

His Appearance

Sri Chaitanya Mahaprabhu was born in Mayapur in the town of Nadia, just after sunset on the evening of the 23rd Phalguna 1407 Sakabda, corresponding to February 18th, 1486 of the Christian Era. The moon was eclipsed at the time of His birth, and the people of Nadia were then engaged, as usual on such occasions, in bathing in the Bhagirathi (Ganges River) with loud cheers of "Haribol!" His father, Jagannath Misra, was a poor Brahmana (priest) of the Vaidic order, and His mother Sachidevi was a woman of ideal character. Both descended from Brahmana families originally residing in Sylhet. Mahaprabhu was a beautiful child, and the ladies of the town came to present Him with gifts. His mother's father, Pandit Nilambar Chakravarti, a renowned astrologer, foretold that the child would be a great personage in time, and he therefore gave Him the name Vishvambhar. The ladies of the neighborhood called Him Gaurahari because of His golden complexion, and His mother called Him Nimai because there was a neem tree near the place where He was born. The boy was very beautiful and everyone loved to see Him every day. As He grew up He became a mischievous and frolicsome lad. After His fifth year He was admitted into a school where He mastered the Bengali language in a very short time.

Most of Lord Chaitanya's contemporary biographers have mentioned certain anecdotes regarding Him, which are simple records of His early miracles. It is said that when He was an infant in His mother's arms, He wept continually, and when the neighboring ladies and His mother cried "Haribol," He would stop. Thus there was a continuation of the utterance of "Haribol" in the house, foretelling the future mission of  the Lord. It has also been stated that when His mother once gave Him sweets to eat, He ate clay instead of the food. When His mother asked for the reason, He stated that as every sweet was nothing but clay transformed, He could eat clay just as well. His mother, who was also the wife of a scholar, explained that every element in a particular state was adapted to a special use. Earth, while in the state of a jug, could be used as a water pot, but in the state of a brick such a use was not possible. Clay, therefore, in the form of sweets was usable as food and not clay in its other states. The lad was convinced and admitted His foolishness in eating the clay and agreed to avoid the mistake in the future.

His Early Pastimes

Another miraculous act has been related. A Brahmana on pilgrimage became a guest in the house of Jagannath Misra. The Brahmana cooked his food and said his grace while meditating on Krishna. In the meantime the lad came and ate up the cooked rice. The Brahmana, astonished at the lad's act, cooked again at the request of Jagannath Misra. The lad again ate up the cooked rice while the Brahmana was offering the rice to Krishna by meditation. The Brahmana was persuaded to cook for the third time. This time, all the residents of the house had fallen asleep and the lad showed Himself as Krishna, the Supreme Personality of Godhead, and he blessed the traveler. The Brahmana was then lost in ecstasy at the appearance of the object of his worship.

It has also been stated that two thieves stole away the lad from His father's door, intending to steal His jewels, and giving Him sweets on the way. The lad exercised His illusory energy however, and directed the thieves back toward His own house. The thieves, for fear of detection, left the boy there and fled.

Another miraculous act has been described of the lad's demanding and getting from Hiranya and Jagadish all the offerings they had collected for worshiping Krishna on the day of Ekadashi. When only four years of age, He sat on rejected cooking pots which were considered unholy by His mother. He explained to His mother that there was no question of holiness or unholiness regarding earthen pots thrown away after the cooking was over. These anecdotes relate to Lord Chaitanya's tender age up to the fifth year.

In His eighth year, He was admitted into the school of Gangadas Pandit in Ganganagar close to the village of Mayapur. In two years He became well read in Sanskrit grammar and rhetoric. His readings after that were of the nature of personal study in His own house where He had found many important books belonging to His father, who was a scholar himself. It appears that He read the *smriti* (scriptures) in His own study and the *nyaya* (logic) also, in competition with His friends, who were then studying under the celebrated Pandit Raghunath Shiromani.

After His tenth year of age, Nimai became a learned scholar in grammar, rhetoric, the *smriti* and the *nyaya*. It was after this that His elder brother Vishvarupa left home and accepted the *ashram* (status) of a *sannyasi* (ascetic). Though a very young boy, Nimai consoled His parents saying that He would serve them with a view to please God. Just after that, His father left this world. His mother was exceedingly aggrieved, and Lord Chaitanya, with His usual contented demeanor, consoled His widowed mother.

It was at the age of fourteen or fifteen that Maha-prabhu was married to Lakshmipriya, the daughter of Ballabhacharya, also of Nadia. By this time Nimai Pandit was considered one of the best scholars of Nadia, which was the renowned seat of *nyaya* philosophy and Sanskrit learning. What to speak of the *smarta* (caste) pandits, the logicians were all afraid of confronting Him in literary discussion.

His Marriage & Social Life

Being a married man, He went to eastern Bengal by the banks of the Padma river for the acquirement of wealth. There He displayed His learning and obtained a good sum of money. It was at this time that He preached Vaishnavism at intervals. After teaching Tapan Mishra the principles of Vaishnavism, He ordered him to go and live in Benares. During His residence in East Bengal, His wife Lakshmipriya left this world from the effects of a snake bite. On returning home, He found His mother in a mourning state. He consoled her by speaking about the uncertainty of human affairs. It was at His mother's request that He married Vishnupriya, the daughter of Raj pandit Sanatan Mishra.

Nimai's comrades joined Him on His return from touring. He was now so renowned that He was considered to be the best pandit in Nadia. Keshava Mishra of Kashmir, who had called himself the Great Digvijayi, came to Nadia to debate with the pandits of that place. Afraid of the so-called conquering pandit, the professors of Nadia left their town on the pretense of another invitation. Keshava Mishra met Nimai at Barokona Ghat in Mayapur, and after a very short discussion he was defeated by the boy, and humiliation obliged him to decamp. Nimai Pandit was now the most important scholar of his time.

At the age of sixteen or seventeen, Lord Chaitanya traveled to Gaya with a host of His students and there took His spiritual initiation from Ishvara Puri, a Vaishnava sannyasi and disciple of the renowned Madhavendra Puri. Upon His return to Nadia, Sri Chaitanya Mahaprabhu began vigorous preaching of the Vaishnava principles. His divine nature became so strongly represented that Adwaita Prabhu, Srivasa Pandit, and others, who had accepted the Vaishnava faith prior to the birth of Lord Chaitanya, were astonished at the change in the young man. He was no longer simply a contentious *naiyaika*, a wrangling *smarta*, or a criticizing rhetorician. He swooned upon hearing the name of Krishna and behaved as an inspired man under the influence of His divine sentiment. It was described by Murari Gupta, an eye-witness, that He showed His divine powers in the house of Srivas Pandit in the presence of hundreds of His followers who were mostly well-read scholars. It was at this time that He opened a nocturnal school of sankirtan (congregational chanting of the Lord's holy names) in the compound of Srivas Pandit with His sincere followers. There He preached, sang, danced, and expressed all sorts of spiritual emotions. Nityananda Prabhu (an incarnation of Balaram, the first expansion of Krishna), who also was a preacher of Vaishnavism and had just completed His travels all over India, joined Him by that time. In fact, a host of pandit preachers of Vaishnavism, all sincere at heart, came and joined Him from different parts of Bengal. Nadia now became the regular seat of a host of Vaishnava *acharyas* (leaders) whose mission it was to spiritualize mankind with the highest influence of the Vaishnava creed.

Mahaprabhu's Mission

The first mandate that Sri Chaitanya Mahaprabhu issued to Nityananda Prabhu and Haridas Thakur was to "Go friends, go through the streets of the town, meet every man at his door, and ask him to sing the name of Hari with devotion, and then come and report to Me every evening the result of your preaching." Thus ordered, the two preachers went on and soon met Jagai and Madhai, two most abominable characters. They insulted the preachers upon hearing Mahaprabhu's mandate,  but were soon converted by the influence of bhakti (devotion to Krishna) inculcated by the Lord Himself. The people of Nadia were now surprised. They said, "Nimai Pandit is not only a great genius, but He is certainly a missionary from God Almighty."

From this time to His twenty-third year, Mahaprabhu

preached His principles not only in Nadia, but in all important towns and villages around His city. In the houses of His followers He performed miracles, taught the esoteric principles of bhakti, and sang His sankirtan with other bhaktas (devotees of Krishna). His followers in the town of Nadia commenced singing the Holy Name of Hari in the streets and marketplaces. This created a sensation and roused different feelings in different circles. The bhaktas were highly pleased. But the Smarta Brahmanas became jealous of Nimai Pandit's success and complained to Chand Kazi, deprecating the character of Sri Chaitanya as un-Hindu. The Kazi came to Srivasa Pandit's house, broke a mridanga (drum), and declared that unless Mahaprabhu ceased making noise about His unorthodox religion, he would be obliged to enforce Mohammedanism on Him and His followers.

This was brought to Mahaprabhu's notice, at which time He ordered the townspeople to appear that evening, each with a torch in their hand. This they did, and Mahaprabhu marched out with his sankirtan party divided into fourteen groups. Upon His arrival at the Kazi's house, He held a long conversation with him and in the end communicated into his heart His Vaishnava influence by touching his body. The Kazi then wept and admitted that he felt a deep spiritual influence that had cleared his doubts and produced in him a religious sentiment which gave him the highest ecstasy. The Kazi then joined the sankirtan party. The world was astonished at the spiritual power of the great Lord, and hundreds and hundreds of heretics converted and joined the banner of Mahaprabhu after this affair.

It was after this that some of the jealous and low-minded

Brahmanas of Kuliya picked a quarrel with Mahaprabhu and
collected a party to oppose Him.

Taking Sannyas

*Mahaprabhu was naturally a soft-hearted person, though
strong in His principles.* He declared that party spirit
and sectarianism were the two great enemies of
progress, and as long as He continued to be an
inhabitant of Nadia belonging to a certain family,
His mission would not meet with complete success.
He then resolved to become a citizen of the world by
cutting off His connection with a particular family, and
with resolution, He took *sannyas* (vows of renunciation)
at Katwa under the guidance of Keshava Bharati of that
town in His twenty-fourth year. His mother and wife
wept bitterly for His separation, but though soft in heart,
Mahaprabhu was a strong person in principle. He left home to
give the unlimited spiritual world of Krishna to all of humanity.

After His *sannyas*, He was asked to visit the house
of Adwaita Prabhu in Shantipur. Sri Adwaita managed to
invite all His friends and admirers from Nadia and brought
Sachidevi to see her son. Both pleasure and pain invaded her
heart when she saw her son in the attire of a sannyasi. As
a sannyasi, Lord Chaitanya wore nothing but a *kaupin* (loin
cloth) and a *bahirbas* (outer covering). His head was shaved,
and His hands bore a *danda* (staff) and a *kamandalu* (ascetic's water pot). The holy son fell at the feet of His beloved
mother and said, "Mother! This body is yours, and I must
obey your orders. Permit Me to go to Vrindavan for My
spiritual attainments." Mother Sachi, in consultation with
Adwaita Prabhu and others, asked her son to reside in
Jagannath Puri, so that she might obtain information about
Him now and then. Mahaprabhu agreed to that proposition,
and in a few days He left Shantipur for Orissa.

His biographers have described the journey of Sri
Krishna Chaitanya (the name He received after taking *san-*

nyas) from Shantipur to Puri in great detail. He traveled along the side of the Bhagirathi river as far as Chattrabog, situated now in Thana Mathurapur, Diamond Harbor, 24 Parganas. There He took a boat and went as far as Prayag Ghat in the Midnapur District. Then He walked through Balasore and Cuttack to Puri, seeing the temple of Bhubaneswar on His way.

Revealing The Ultimate Truth

Upon His arrival at Puri, He saw Lord Jagannath in the temple and visited Sarvabhauma Bhattacharya at his request. Sarvabhauma was a great pandit of the day. His knowledge knew no bounds. He was the best *naiyaika* (logician) of his time, and was known as the most erudite scholar in the Vedanta philosophy of the school of Shankaracharya. He was born in Nadia (Vidyanagar) and taught innumerable pupils the *nyaya* philosophy in his school there. He had gone to reside in Puri some time before the birth of Nimai Pandit.

His brother-in-law, Gopinath Misra, introduced the new sannyasi to Sarvabhauma, who was astonished at His personal beauty, and feared that it would be difficult for the young man to maintain His *sannyas* vows for the duration of His life. Gopinath, who had known Mahaprabhu from Nadia, had great reverence for Him, and stated that the sannyasi was not a common human being. On this point Gopinath and Sarvabhauma had a heated discussion. Sarvabhauma then requested Mahaprabhu to hear his recitation of the *Vedanta Sutras*, to which He tacitly submitted.

Lord Chaitanya heard with silence what the great Sarvabhauma gravely spoke for seven days, at the end of which the Bhattacharya said, "Krishna Chaitanya! I think You do not understand the Vedanta, as You have not said anything after hearing my recitation and explanations." Lord Chaitanya replied that He understood the sutras very well, but He could not make out what Shankaracharya meant by his commentaries. Astonished at this, Sarvabhauma said, "How

is it that You understand the meanings of the sutras, yet
You do not understand the commentaries which explain the
sutras? Very well. If You understand the sutras, please let me
have Your interpretations."

Mahaprabhu thereon explained all the sutras in His own
way, without touching on the pantheistic commentary of
Shankara. With his keen understanding, Sarvabhauma saw
the truth, beauty, and harmony of the explanations given by
Lord Chaitanya, and he was obliged to admit that it was the
first time he had found anyone who could explain the *Brahma
Sutras* in such a simple manner. He admitted also that he
felt the commentaries of Shankara never gave such natural
explanations of the *Vedanta Sutras* as he had obtained from
Mahaprabhu. He then submitted himself as Mahaprabhu's
advocate and follower. Within a few days, Sarvabhauma
became one of the best Vaishnavas of the time. When news
of this spread, all of Orissa sang the praises of Sri Krishna
Chaitanya, and hundreds and hundreds of people came to
Him and became His followers.

Some time later, Mahaprabhu visited southern India,
accompanied on His journey by one Brahmana named
Krishna Das. His biographers have given us details of the
journey. He first went to Kurmakshetra, where He performed
a miracle by curing a leper named Vasudeva. From there, He
met with Ramananda Raya, the governor of Vidyanagar, on
the banks of the Godavari, and had a philosophical conversation with him on the subject of *prema bhakti*. He performed
another miracle by touching the seven Tal trees and making
them immediately disappear. It was through these trees that
Lord Sri Ramachandra had shot His arrow and killed the
great king Vali. Mahaprabhu preached Vaishnavism and *nama
sankirtan* throughout the entire journey.

At Rangakshetra, He stayed for four months in the house
of Venkata Bhatta during the rainy season. There He converted the whole family of Venkata from Ramanuja Vaishnavas

into Krishna bhaktas, along with the son of Venkata, a boy of ten years named Gopal, who afterward came to Vrindavan and became one of the six Goswamis or prophets serving under their leader Sri Krishna Chaitanya. Trained in Sanskrit by his uncle Prabodhananda Saraswati, Gopal Bhatta wrote several books on Vaishnavism.

Lord Chaitanya visited numerous places in South India as far as Cape Comorin, and returned to Puri in two years by Panderpur on the Bhima river. In this latter place He spiritualized Tukaram, who from that time became a religious preacher himself. (This fact has been admitted in the *abhangas* of Tukaram which have been collected in a volume by Mr. Satyendranath Tagore of the Bombay Civil Service.) Also along His journey He had discussions with Buddhists, Jains, and Mayavadis in several places, and converted His opponents to Vaishnavism. Upon His return to Puri, King Prataparudra and several pandit Brahmanas joined under the banner of Sri Chaitanya Mahaprabhu.

His Topmost Assistants

In His twenty-eighth year, Mahaprabhu went into Bengal as far as Gauda in Maldah. There He picked up two great persons named Rupa and Sanatan. Though descended from the lineage of the Karnatic Brahmanas, these two brothers were essentially considered Muslims due to their continual association with Hussain Shah, the emperor of Gauda. Their names had been changed by the emperor to Dabir Khas and Sakar Mallik, and their master loved them dearly, as they were both learned in Persian, Arabic, and Sanskrit and were loyal servants of the state. The two gentlemen had found no way to return to Hinduism and had written to Mahaprabhu for spiritual help while He was at Puri. Mahaprabhu had written in reply that He would come to them and extricate them from their spiritual difficulties. Now that He had come to Gauda, both the brothers appeared before Him with their long-stand-ing prayer. Mahaprabhu ordered them to go to Vrindavan and meet Him there.

Lord Chaitanya returned to Puri through Shantipur where He again met His dear mother. After a short stay at Puri, He left for Vrindavan. This time He was accompanied by one devotee named Balabhadra Bhattacharya. He visited Vrindavan and came down to Prayag (Allahabad), converting a large number of Mohammedans into Vaishnavas using arguments from the Koran. The descendents of those Vaishnavas are still known today as Pathan Vaishnavas.

At Allahabad, Rupa Goswami met with Lord Chaitanya, who trained him up in spirituality in ten days and directed him to go to Vrindavan on two missions. His first mission was to write theological works scientifically explaining pure bhakti and *prema*. The second mission was to revive the places where Sri Krishnachandra had, at the end of *Dvapara-yuga* (a previous age) exhibited His spiritual lila (pastimes) for the benefit of the world.

After Rupa Goswami left Allahabad for Vrindavan, Mahaprabhu went to Benares. There He stayed at the house of Chandrashekar and accepted His daily *bhiksha* (alms) in the house of Tapan Misra. It was here that Sanatan Goswami joined Him and took instruction in spiritual matters for two months. The biographers, especially Krishnadas Kaviraj, have given us the details of Lord Chaitanya's teachings to Rupa and Sanatan. Krishnadas Kaviraj was not a contemporary writer, but he gathered his information from the Goswamis themselves, who were the direct disciples of Mahaprabhu. Jiva Goswami, who was the nephew of Sanatan and Rupa, and who has left us his invaluable work the *Sat-sandarbha*, has philosophized on the precepts of his great leader. We have gathered and summarized the precepts of Sri Chaitanya from the books of those great writers.

While in Benares, Lord Chaitanya had an interview with the learned sannyasis of that town in the house of a Maharastrian Brahmana, who had invited all the sannyasis for a discussion. At this interview, Mahaprabhu exhibited His spiritual effulgence, which attracted all the sannyasis to Him. Then a conversation ensued. The sannyasis were headed by their most learned leader, Prakashananda Saraswati. After a short controversy, they submitted to Lord Chaitanya and admitted that they had been misled by the commentaries of Shankaracharya. It was impossible even for learned scholars to oppose Lord Chaitanya, as there was something special in Him that touched their hearts and made them weep for their spiritual improvement. The sannyasis of Benares soon fell at the feet of Lord Chaitanya and asked for His *kripa* (mercy). Lord Chaitanya then preached pure bhakti and instilled into their hearts spiritual love for Krishna, which obliged them to give up sectarian feelings. On this wonderful conversion of the sannyasis, the whole of Benares became Vaishnavas, and they all performed sankirtan with their new Lord.

After sending Sanatan to Vrindavan, Mahaprabhu again went to Puri, traveling through the jungle with His comrade Balabhadra. Balabhadra reported that Mahaprabhu had exhibited many miracles on His way to Puri, such as making tigers and elephants dance upon hearing the name of Krishna.

From His thirty-first year, Mahaprabhu continually lived in Puri at the house of Kasi Misra, until His disappearance in His forty-eighth year at the time of sankirtan in the temple of Tota Gopinath. During these eighteen years, His life was one of settled love and devotion. He was surrounded by numerous followers, all of whom were of the highest order of Vaishnavas, distinguished from the common people by their pure charac-ter and learning, firm religious principles, and spiritual love for Radha and Krishna.

Svarup Damodar, who had been known by the name of Purushottamacharya while Mahaprabhu was in Nadia, joined Him from Benares and engaged in His service as His secretary. No production of any poet or philosopher

could be laid before Mahaprabhu unless Svarup Damodar
had acknowledged it as pure and useful. Ramananda Raya
was the second of His most intimate confidants. Both he and
Svarup Damodar sang while Mahaprabhu expressed His sentiments on a certain point of worship. Paramananda Puri
was His minister of religion.

Mahaprabhu slept little. His sentiments carried Him farther and farther into the firmament of spirituality every day
and night, and all His admirers and followers observed Him
throughout. He worshiped, communicated with His mission-
aries at Vrindavan, and conversed with those religious men
who had newly come to visit Him. He sang and danced, taking
no care of Himself, and often lost Himself in religious beatitude. All who came to Him saw Him as the all-beautiful God
appearing in the material world for the benefit of mankind.
He lovingly remembered His mother all along, and sent her
mahaprasad (food offered to the Lord) now and then with
those who went to Nadia. He was most amiable in nature
and humility was personified in Him. His sweet appearance
brought joy to all who came in contact with Him.

Lord Chaitanya appointed Nityananda Prabhu as the
missionary in charge of Bengal. He dispatched six disciples
(the Goswamis) to Vrindavan to preach in the upcountry. He
punished all of His disciples who deviated from holy life.
This He markedly did in the case of Chota (junior) Haridas.
He never failed to give proper instructions in life to those
who solicited them. This was seen in His teachings to
Raghunath das Goswami. His treatment of
Haridas (senior) showed how He loved godly
men and how He defied caste distinctions in
the face of spiritual brotherhood.

His Precepts

The Precepts
of Sri Chaitanya Mahaprabhu

"Give up the shackles of material life slowly. Cultivate your spiritual consciousness internally. Give up prejudices that you have acquired from the so-called rational thinkers who deny the existence of spirit. Be humble and learn to respect those who work toward spiritual attainments..."

Lord Chaitanya teaches us first that the rational attributes of people are not capable of approaching the divine sphere of spirit. He considers reason to be quite incompetent in such a matter. However, He considers that the religious sentiment in man, even in a very small quantity, does have the power to comprehend spirit. Inspiration alone can give light to spiritual matters. Inspiration coming down from the higher realm through purified and blessed souls has been exhibited in the form of the *Vedas*. The *Vedas*, together with their explanatory notes, the *Puranas*, are therefore the only evidence in matters of spirit, and are eternal in nature. Thus, Vedic truths should be accepted as the only truth in higher matters. Reason, while sincerely helping the inspired truth, may be accepted as auxiliary evidence. According to Lord Chaitanya, the *Vedas* teach us nine principal doctrines:

1. Hari (the Almighty) is one without a second.

2. He is always vested with infinite power.

3. He is an ocean of rasa (sweetness).

4. The soul is His vibhinnangsha, or separated part.

5. Certain souls are engrossed by prakriti, or His illusory energy.

6. Certain souls are released from the grasp of prakriti.

7. All spiritual and material phenomena are the achintya-bhedabheda-prakash of Hari, the Almighty.

8. Bhakti is the only means of attaining the final objective of spiritual existence.

9. Krishna prema alone is the final object of spiritual existence.

Hari, The Almighty One

1

In Vedic theology, the creative principle of the Deity is personified in Brahma and the destructive principle in Shiva. Indra is the head of some of the lower elements of administration. Hence, they are not the Almighty Himself, but are different representations of different attributes of the Almighty. They have obtained their powers from an original fountainhead. Thus, they are subordinate beings in the service of Hari. Then again there are three distinct philosophical ideas of the Deity: (1) the idea of the all-pervading Brahman of the pantheistic school, (2) the idea of a universal soul (Paramatma) of the yoga school, and (3) the idea of a personal God (Bhagavan) with all His majesty, might, glory, beauty, wisdom, and supremacy combined in His personality. The ideas of Brahman and Paramatma are, therefore, included in the idea of Bhagavan. Thus, Bhagavan is Hari, the Supreme Being.

Human ideas are either mental or spiritual. The mental idea is defective, as it has its relation to the created principle of matter. The spiritual idea is certainly the nearest approach to the Supreme Being. Then again, the spiritual idea of Bhagavan is of two kinds. In one kind, the person of the Almighty is overpowered by His majesty, and in the other, His personal beauty overpowers all His majesty. The first idea is represented in the great Narayan of Vaikuntha, who is the Lord of lords and God of gods. The second is represented in the all-beautiful Krishna with Radhika, who is the representative of His *hladini* or superior ecstatic energy.

Krishna appears as a man among men, yet is generally accepted as God above gods. Krishna attracts, loves, and produces ecstasy in all souls. His qualities and personal paraphernalia are all purely spiritual, and have no relation to the material world. The material senses of man cannot approach Him. It is the spirit in man which can see Him directly and commune with Him. The soul fettered in matter has, from its own degradation, lost its right to see Krishna and His spiritual lila in the spiritual world, but Krishna may, out of His own supreme power and prerogative, appear with all His Vrindavan lila before the eyes of all men. The rational man can hardly conceive of or believe in Krishna and His lila, but as man's spiritual vision improves, he sees Krishna and loves Him with all his heart. This subject can hardly be explained fully and exhaustively. We therefore leave this point to our readers with these words: "Give up the shackles of material life slowly. Cultivate your spiritual consciousness internally. Give up prejudices that you have acquired from the so-called rational thinkers who deny the existence of spirit. Be humble and learn to respect those who work toward spiritual attainments. Do this with your heart, mind, and strength in the company of Vaishnavas alone, and you will see Krishna in no time. Krishna is not an imaginary being, nor have you a right to think that He is a material phenomenon fancied to be the Supreme Being by fools. Krishna is not understood by the process of distinguishing the subjective from the objective, nor is He to be accepted as an imposition on the people set up by self-interested men. Krishna is eternal, spiritually true, reflected on the human soul relieved of all attachment to dull matter, and is the subject of love which proceeds from the soul. Accept Him as such, and you will see Him with your soul's eyes."

Words fail to describe the Transcendental Being. The highest, best, and most spiritual ideal of the Divinity is to be found in Krishna. To bring arguments against Him is simply to deceive one's self, and deprive one's self of the blessings that God has kept in store for man. Hence, all descriptions of His name, form, attributes, and lila should be accepted spiritually, giving up the material conceptions which words must necessarily convey.

2 Hari Has Infinite Powers

Infinite powers means powers that know no bounds either in space or in time. As God's powers alone created space and time, His powers are identical to Himself. In material life, there is a difference between a person and his powers, between a thing and its attributes, its name, its form, and its activities; but it is a spiritual truth that in spirit, a person is identical with his name, form, attributes, and activities. This truth cannot be subjected to dry reason which deals with gross matter alone. Krishna is the supreme will in Himself, and He exercises His supreme power at His pleasure, which submits to no law, because all law has proceeded from His will and power.

Power is known by its exercise. In this world we have experience of only three of the attributes of God's power. We see the material phenomena and we understand that His power has the attribute to create matter. This attribute is known in the Vedas as *maya-shakti*. We see a man and we understand that the Supreme Power has the attribute to produce the limited and imperfect souls. The *shastras* (scriptures) call that attribute *jiva-shakti*. We conceive of One who is spiritual and supreme in His realm of eternal spirits; thus, we understand that His power has an attribute to exhibit perfectly spiritual existences. The Vedas call that attribute by the name of *atma-shakti* or *chit-shakti*.

All these attributes together form one supreme power which the Vedas call *para-shakti*. In fact, power (*shakti*) is not distinguishable from the personality of that Supreme Being. Still, the powers are separately exhibited in their separate actions. This is styled *achintya-bhedabheda-prakash* or inconceivable, simultaneous existence of distinction and non-distinction. Hari, being the Supreme Will above law, exercises His infinite powers while He Himself remains unaffected. This is not understood by reason, but felt in the soul as an intuitive truth.

He Is An Ocean Of Sweetness

3

Rasa has been defined as that ecstatic principle that comprehends sthayi-bhava, vibhava, anubhava, sattvik, and sanchari. Vibhava is divided into *alambana* and *uddipana. Alambana* is subdivided into *vishaya* and *ashraya. Ashraya* is that person who has in himself the principle of *sthayi-bhava*, and *vishaya* is that person to whom the *stayi-bhava* directs itself. *Sthayi-bhava* has been explained to be *rati* or the tendency of the pure spiritual heart. By a connection of *ashraya* and *vishaya* the *sthayi-bhava* arrives at its stage of action. When it obtains its active stage, certain signs are exhibited in the person which are called the *anubhavas*. These are thirteen in number. Eight other *bhavas* exhibited in the body are known as *sattvik-bhavas*, such as tears, shivering, etc. Thirty-three other *bhavas*, such as *harsha, vishad*, etc. have been shown to be *sanchari-bhavas*. These combined in the soul form the *rasa*.

This process of exhibition of *rasa* relates to the exhibition of rasa in the person enthralled by matter. But *rasa* itself is an eternal principle identified with the Supreme, Hari. Hari is the ocean of *rasa*, and in the human soul only a drop of that ocean could be conceived. *Rasa* naturally is spiritual, but in man subjected to maya, the progenitor of matter, it has been identified in a perverted state with the sensual pleasure of man in connection with material objects. In this condition, the soul loses itself in the mind, and the mind acting through the senses enjoys the perverted reflection of rasa in the five different kinds of objects of the five senses. This is the soul's going abroad with *avidya*, or ignorance of the spiritual self. When the soul looks inward, it obtains its spiritual rasa, and the perverted *rasa* wanes off in proportion to the development of the spiritual *rasa*.

In spiritual *rasa*, the souls with each other and with the all-beautiful Lord have their unfettered action in Vrindavan, rising above material time and space. Hari, with His infinite supreme free will, has eternal ecstasy in His spiritual power or *chit-shakti*. The *hladini* attribute of *chit-shakti* (spiritual wisdom) gives Him infinite pleasure. The *samvit* attribute of *chit-shakti* produces all *bhavas*, relations, and affections. The *sandhini* attribute of *chit-shakti* produces all existence (other than the free will), including the *dhams* (abodes), individualities, and other substances in connection with the action of the spiritual rasa. All these exhibitions are from *chit-shakti* or the spiritual power.

In spiritual rasa, the souls with each other and with the all-beautiful Lord have their unfettered action in Vrindavan, rising above material time and space.

The mayik or material creation, including time, space, and gross objects, has no place in *chit-jagat* or the spiritual world, which is the same as Vrindavan. *Maya-shakti* is a perverted reflection of the *chit-shakti*. Hence, the qualities in the *mayik-jagat* (material world) resemble the qualities in the *chit-jagat* (spiritual universe), but are not substantially the same. The *chit-jagat* is the model of the *mayik-jagat*, but they are not identical. We must guard ourselves against the idea that man has imagined *chit-jagat* from an experience of the *mayik-jagat*. This idea is pantheistic, and it may also be styled atheistic. Reason not spiritualized has a tendency to create such a doubt, but one who has a wish to enjoy spiritual love must give it up as misleading. The eternal rasa of Krishna exists spiritually in *chit-jagat*. To us who are in the relative world, there is a screen which intervenes between our eyes and the great spiritual scene of Krishna lila. When by the grace of Krishna that screen is drawn up, we have the privilege to see it, and again when it pleases the Almighty to drop the screen, the great Vrindavan lila disappears. "Taste the subject and your conviction will be the same as mine. Brethren, do not give up such an important subject without liberal examination!"

The Soul
Is His Separated Part

4

By "soul," the Vedic literatures refer to all sorts of souls, whether animal, human, or celestial. It must be understood that Mahaprabhu taught the very liberal principle of transmigration (reincarnation) of the soul. Although certain readers may reject this idea on the grounds that certain forms of faith do not support this theory, it is not prudent to reject a theory because it differs with the dogmas of certain sectarian creeds. Indeed, it is a matter that reason cannot dare to meddle with. Candidly examining, we cannot find any strong reason to disbelieve the theory of transmigration. Rather,

our unprejudiced mind is inclined to accept it.

The belief that the human soul has only one trial in life is evidently dogmatic, unjust, and contrary to the belief that God is all good. When our spiritual sentiment supports the Vedic conclusions, which have taught us the facts about continual existence of the soul in different stages of creation, we must give up the idea of disbelieving in the principle of transmigration of the soul. However educated and scientific a man may be, he is always liable to a creeping error, and that error may even be supported by an entire sect or nation.

The soul, according to Chaitanya Mahaprabhu, is an atomic part of the Divine Soul. It is a part of God's power to produce beings who are spiritual in essence, but liable to be enthralled by maya (illusion) when they forget their position as eternal servants of the Supreme. God here is compared with the sun, and the souls are said to be the atomic portions of that sun's rays, unable to stand freely unless they are protected by another attribute of God's power. The word "part" is not meant in the same way as to describe portions cut out of a piece of stone by an axe, but should be understood by the example of one lamp lit from another, or gold produced from an alchemical stone.

The souls are also compared with separate atomic sparks of a burning fire. Each soul has drawn from its fountain-head a proportionate share of the attributes of the Supreme, and consequently, a small proportion of the free will. These souls are naturally located between the *chit-jagat* and *mayik-jagat*. Those who chose to serve their God were protected from falldown by the interference of the *hladini* attribute of the Supreme's *chit-shakti*. They have been admitted as eternal servants of the Lord in various ways. They know not the troubles of maya and the *karma-chakra*, or the rotative principles of mayik action and its result. Those who wanted to enjoy were captured by maya from the other side. They are in Maya's *karma-chakra*, ending only when they again see their original position as servants of the Supreme Lord. These souls, whether liberated from Maya's charm or enthralled by her, are separate responsible beings depending on the Supreme, Hari.

Hari is the Lord of Maya; she serves Him at His pleasure. The soul or jiva is so constructed as to be liable to be enthralled by maya when unassisted by the *hladini shakti* of the Lord. Hence, there is a natural and inherent distinction between God and the *jiva* that no pantheistic maneuver can annihilate. Please avoid the misleading question, "When were these *jivas* created and enthralled?" The mayik time has no existence in spiritual history because it has its commencement after the enthrallment of *jivas* in matter; one cannot, therefore, employ mayik chronology in matters like these.

The Soul Captured By Illusion

5

Prakriti, maya, pradhan, prapancha, and avidya are different names of the same principle according to its different phases and attributes. Maya is not an independent *shakti* from the supreme svarup-shakti. She is simply a devotee serving God executing His orders to reform those who become ungrateful to Him. Maya is in charge of God's house of correction, and her energy is a reflection of God's supreme power. Those *jivas* who, in abusing their free will, forgot that they were eternal servants of the Lord and thought of enjoying for themselves, were captured by Maya for their penal servitude and correction.

Maya has three attributes: *sattva*, *rajas*, and *tamas*. Those attributes are just like chains used to bind the ungrateful souls. Maya then applies a double casing on the spiritual form of the soul. The casing is described by the words *linga* and *sthul*. The mayik existence has twenty-four substances. The five elements (earth, water, fire, air, and ether), the five properties (sound, touch, sight, taste, and smell), the five knowledge-acquiring senses (eye, ear, nose, tongue, and skin), and the five working senses (the hands, legs, speech, genital, and organ for evacuation); these twenty form the *sthul* or outer-casing. The mind, intelligence, contaminated consciousness, and false ego comprise the *linga-deha* or inner-casing. Then, after encasing the spiritual form of the soul, Maya employs the fallen souls in different kinds of work. Mayik work is composed of *karma*, *akarma*, and *vikarma*. Karma is con-  ventially good action done to obtain *punya* or virtue, such as performance of duties enjoined by the *varnashram* dharma of the Smartas. Karma elevates one to the heav- enly realm. *Akarma* (failure to perform one's duty) places one in an unpleasant state on Earth, and *vikarma* (sinful or criminal actions) hurls souls down to hellish life. The fallen souls travel from body to body with their *linga-deha*, doing karma or *vikarma*, rising up to the heavens and again coming down at the exhaustion of their virtues, going down to hell, and after suffering punishment, again rising up to the platform of fruitive work. Thus, the state of the fallen souls is deplor- able to the extreme degree, as they sometimes suffer mas- sacre and murder, and sometimes enjoy as princes. The material world is, therefore, a prison or a house of correc- tion, and not a place for enjoyment, as some people assert.

The Soul Released From Illusion

6

Jivas are traveling on the path of mayik existence from time immemorial, experiencing all sorts of plea- sure and pain. How can one become free from this unpleasant condition? Religious rituals, performance of duty, yoga, development of powers of the body and the mind, *sankhya* (empiric philosophical analysis), simple knowledge that one is a spiritual being, and *vairagya*, giving up all enjoyments in the world, are not the proper means by which one can actually achieve what he or she genuinely wants. When a person comes in contact with a Vaishnava whose heart has been melted by *hari-bhakti-rasa*, it is then that he or she may desire to imbibe the sweet prin-

ciple of bhakti and follow in the holy footsteps of the devotee by constantly practicing krishna-bhakti. They slowly wash off the mayik condition, and in the end, after obtaining their true nature, enjoy the sweetest unalloyed *rasa*, which is the ultimate attainment of the soul.

Satsanga, or the company of spiritual people, is the only means to obtain the ultimate object of life. Bhakti is a principle which comes from soul to soul, and like electricity or magnetism in gross matter, it conducts itself from one congenial soul to another. The principle of bhakti is sincere, entire dependence on the Supreme Lord in every act of life. The principle of duty is not part of bhakti, as it acts on the basis of gratitude for favors obtained, and it involves obligation, which is contrary to natural love.

The principle of morality in the mortal world, though good in its own way, scarcely brings spiritual results in the end. Faith in the supreme beauty of the Lord, a desire for the eternal unselfish service of that Supreme Being, and a consequent repulsion of every other thought of pleasure or self-aggrandizement are the three principles which constitute *sraddha*, or actual hankering after bhakti. Bhakti by nature is *ananya* or exclusive. Is it chance, then, which brings bhakti? No, *sukriti* or good work is the prime moving principle. Good work is of two types. One type, passing as morality, includes those works that bring virtue and aggrandizement. The other type of good work includes all activities that have a tendency to bring about spiritual progress. This latter type of good work or *sukriti* brings one in contact with a sincere Vaishnava from whom one can initially imbibe *sraddha* or faith in spirit; and being then capable of receiving bhakti,

one obtains the seed of devotional service from that
Vaishnava, who is actually the person's guru.

7 Unity In Diversity

Metaphysical discussions are perfectly useless.
The Vedas sometimes establish that the *jiva* is distinct
from the Lord, and sometimes the *jiva* is the same
as the Lord. Factually, the *Vedas* always tell the truth.
The *jiva* is simultaneously distinct from and identical
with God (*achintya-bhedabheda-prakash*). This is not
understood by the rationalist. Hence, it must be said that
in the exercise of His powers beyond human comprehen-
sion, God is distinct from the jiva and the world, and yet
identical with them at all times. The Vedanta teaches us
the *shakti-parinamvad*, and not the erroneous *vivartavad* of
Shankaracharya. Shankara's teachings are explained in different ways. Some say that the world and the *jiva* have
emanated from God, and others establish that the *jiva* and
the world are but developments of the Godhead. Shankara,
in order to avoid *brahma-parinam* (transformation of the
Godhead into the world) theorizes that Srila Vyasadeva
teaches us *vivartavad* (that God undergoes no change whatso-
ever, but it is maya that covers a part of the Supreme, just
as a pot encloses a part of the sky); or that God is reflected
on *avidya* or ignorance, while in fact nothing other than God
has yet come into existence.

These are worthless and abstruse arguments. It is plain
that the Vedanta teaches us that God is unchangeable and is
never subject to modifications. His power alone creates the
jiva and the material world by its own *parinam* (modification).
The example is in the action of the alchemist's stone, the
power of which comes in the form of gold while the stone
remains unchanged. Thus, *chit-shakti* appears in the form
of the *chit-jagat*, with all its particularities of eternal *rasa*,
and *jiva-shakti* appears in the form of the innumerable
jivas, some staying in Vaikuntha as *parishads* or "angels,"

and others moving in this world in various shapes and forms under very different circumstances. *Maya-shakti* creates numerous worlds for the habitations and entertainments of the fallen souls.

Vivartavad is no doubt an error and is quite opposed to the teachings of the Vedas, whereas *shakti-parinamvad* alone is true and supports the fact that spiritual love is eternal. If *vivartavad* were true, the natural consequence would be to declare spiritual love to be a temporary principle.

Bhakti Is The Only Means

8

Karma alone cannot directly and immediately produce a spiritual result. When it does, it does so by means of bhakti. Hence, bhakti is independent, and karma and *jnana* are dependent principles. *Jnana*, or the knowledge that man is a spiritual being, cannot directly bring the ultimate result. When it does, it does so with the assistance of bhakti. Bhakti, therefore, is the only means to obtain the ultimate goal. Bhakti is thus defined as the cultivation of a friendly sentiment for Krishna, free from all desires other than those for the sentiment's own improvements, and unalloyed by such other ingredients as karma and *jnana*, etc. It will be seen that bhakti is itself both a feeling and an action. Bhakti has three stages: *sadhana-bhakti, bhava-bhakti,* and *prema-bhakti. Sadhana-bhakti* is that stage of culture when the feeling of love for Krishna has not yet been aroused. In *bhava-bhakti* the feeling awakens, and in *prema-bhakti* the feeling is fully set into action. Bhakti is a spiritual feeling toward the spiritual object of love.

Sadhana-bhakti is of two kinds: one is called *vaidhi-sadhana-bhakti*, and the other is called *raganuga-sadhana-bhakti*. The word "*vaidhi*" is from "*vidhi*," or "rule." *Vaidhi-bhakti* is practiced by following the rules of the *shastras* as long as feeling is not aroused, whereas in *raganuga-bhakti*, one out of natural tendency loves Krishna, and there is a strong desire to serve the Lord of the heart. One who is charmed by the beauty of this process is quickly able to cultivate his feeling for Krishna; but of the two, *raganuga-bhakti* is stronger than *vaidhi-bhakti*.

Cultivation of the friendly feelings for Krishna is performed in nine different ways:

1. *Hearing of the spiritual name, form, attributes, and lila of Krishna.*
2. *Speaking about and singing the glories of all those.*
3. *Meditating on and remembering all those.*
4. *Serving His holy feet.*
5. *Worshiping.*
6. *Bowing down.*
7. *Doing all that pleases Him.*
8. *Developing friendship toward Him.*
9. *Complete surrender to Him.*

Of all these processes, kirtan, or singing the name of Krishna, is the best.

Humble knowledge is necessary in these types of worship, and fruitless discussions must be avoided. There are some who object to the idea of worshiping *Srimurti* (the Deity form of Krishna). They say, "It is idolatry to worship *Srimurti*. *Srimurti* is an idol formed by an artist and introduced by no one other than Satan himself. Worshiping such an object would arouse the jealousy of God and limit His omnipotence, omniscience, and omnipresence!"

To this we reply, "Brethren! Candidly understand the question and do not allow yourself to be misled by sectarian dogmas. God is not jealous, as He is one without a second. Satan is none other than an object of the imagination or the subject of an allegory. An allegorical or imaginary being should not be allowed to act as an obstacle to bhakti."

Those who believe God to be impersonal simply identify Him with some power or attribute in nature, though in fact He is above nature, her laws, and her rules. His holy wish is law and it would be sacrilege to confine His unlimited excellence by identifying Him with attributes which may exist in created objects such as time, space, etc. His excellence lies in His having mutually contradicting powers and attributes ruled by His supernatural Self.

He is identical with His all-beautiful form, having such powers as omnipresence, omniscience, and omnipotence, the like of which cannot be found elsewhere. His holy and perfect personality exists eternally in the spiritual world, and at the same time exists in every created object and place in all its fullness. This idea excels all other ideas of the Deity. Mahaprabhu rejects idolatry, yet considers the worship of *Srimurti* to be the only unexceptionable means of spiritual culture.

It has been shown that God is personal and all beautiful. Sages like Vyasadeva and others have seen that beauty in their soul's eyes and left us descriptions. Of course, words carry the grossness of matter; but truth is still perceivable in those descriptions. According to those descriptions, one delineates a *Srimurti* and sees the great God of our heart there with intense pleasure. Brethren! Is that wrong or sinful?

Those who say that God has no form, either material or spiritual, and at the same time imagine a false form for worship, are certainly idolatrous. But those who see the spiritual form of the Deity in their soul's eyes carry that impression as far as possible to the mind, and then frame an

emblem for the satisfaction of the material eye
for continual study of the higher feeling, are by
no means idolatrous. While seeing a *Srimurti*, do
not even see the image itself, but see the spiritual
model of the image and you are a pure theist.
Idolatry and *Srimurti* worship are two different things!
But my brethren, you simply confuse one with the other
out of hastiness.

To tell you the truth, *Srimurti* worship is the only true
worship of the Deity, without which you cannot sufficiently cultivate your religious feelings. The world attracts you through
your senses, and as long as you do not see God in the
objects of your senses, you live in an awkward position, which
scarcely helps you in procuring your spiritual elevation. Place
a *Srimurti* in your house. Think that God Almighty is the guardian of the house. Offer food to Him and take it as His *prasada*
(mercy). Flowers and scents should also be offered to Him and
accepted as *prasada*. The eye, ear, nose, skin, and tongue all
have a spiritual culture. You do it with a holy heart and God
will know it and judge you by your sincerity. Satan will have
nothing to do with you in that matter!

All sorts of worship are based on the principle of *Srimurti*.
Look into the history of religion and you will come to this
noble truth. The Semitic idea of a patriarchal God, both in the
pre-Christian period of Judaism and period of Christianity
thereafter, and Mohammedanism, are nothing but limited
ideas of *Srimurti*. The monarchic idea of a Jove among the
Greeks and of an Indra among the Aryan *karma-kandis* is also
a distant view of the same principle. The ideas of a force and
Jyotirmaya Brahma of the meditators, and a formless energy
of the Shaktas are also very faint views of the *Srimurti*.

In fact, the principle of *Srimurti* is the truth itself differ-
ently exhibited in different people according to their different phases of thought. Even Jaimini and Comte, who are not
prepared to accept a creating God, have prescribed focusing

on certain aspects of the *Srimurti*, simply because they have
been impelled by some inward action from the soul! And of
course, we meet with people who have adopted the Cross, the
Shalagram-shila, the *Shiva-lingam*, and other such emblems
as indicators of the inward idea of *Srimurti*.

Furthermore, if divine compassion, love, and justice
could be portrayed by the pencil and expressed by the chisel,
then why shouldn't the personal beauty of the Deity be portrayed in poetry or in picture or expressed by the chisel for
the benefit of man? If words can impress thoughts, a watch
can indicate time, and a sign can tell us a history, then
why can't a picture or figure bring associations of higher
thoughts and feelings related to the transcendental beauty of
the Supreme Lord?

Srimurti worshipers are divided into two classes: the ideal
and the physical. Those of the physical school are obliged
from their circumstances of life and state of mind to establish
temple institutions. Those who are by circumstances and position entitled to worship the *Srimurti* within the mind have,
with due deference to the temple institutions, a tendency to
worship usually by *sravana* (hearing) and kirtan (glori-
fying), and their church is universal and independent
of considerations of caste and color. Mahaprabhu pre-
ferred this latter class, and exemplified their worship
in his *Shikshastaka*. Worship, then, without interrup-
tion in a mood of surrender, and in a very short time
you will be blessed with prema.

Krishna Prema Is The Goal

9 *The karma-margis declare that enjoyment in this
world and in the heavens hereafter* is all that a man
requires. Karma, or action, is of two types: karma
done with a view to obtain a material result, and karma done
with a view to please God. To the *karma-margis*, both types
of karma have the object of procuring enjoyment. God is
worshiped simply to grant material enjoyment. Here is the

line of demarcation between bhakti and karma. Bhakti aims
at procuring the principle of *priti* or divine love as the final
result of all actions, while karma aims at selfish enjoyment
as the ultimate goal of action.

The *jnana-margis*, on the other hand, cultivate *jnana* or
spiritual knowledge to obtain *mukti* or salvation as the final
aim of their cultivation. *Mukti* is defined to
be of two kinds. In one kind of *mukti*, total
absorption of the soul in God is effected,
bringing about the annihilation of the separate existence of the soul from God. This is
known as *sayujya*. In the other kind of *mukti*,
the soul stands eternally distinct from God,
and when salvation ensues, the soul goes to the spiritual
world, obtaining either: *salokya* or residence in the kingdom of God; *samipya* or close association with the Lord;
sarupya or attainment of a spiritual form like that of God
Himself; or *sarshti*, the attainment of powers similar to
the powers of God.

The latter class of *mukti* is inevitable when it pleases the
Almighty to grant us that state. But then after obtaining that
mukti, we serve God with *priti* or pure love. The first kind of
mukti is rejected by the bhaktas as not worth having because
of its tendency to annihilate the highest principle of love. The
second type of *mukti* cannot be the ultimate objective, as it
acts like an intermediate condition of the soul, *priti* there
acting as the ultimatum. *Mukti* therefore must be treated as an
intermediate result of our spiritual disenchantment.

Besides that, a hankering after *mukti* spoils the action of
spiritual cultivation, since it is a strong desire for something
other than the improvement of bhakti. It has a tint of selfish-
ness which is not in keeping with the unselfish principle of
pure bhakti. We must therefore cultivate bhakti, being always
free from the two contending forces, i.e., a desire for *bhukti*,
or selfish enjoyment, and a desire for *mukti*, or salvation. We

must depend on Krishna to either give us *mukti* or not as it pleases Him. We must pray for continual development of our religious sentiment, or bhakti alone. *Priti*, or pure love, is the final object of our existence.

Rati, as explained above, is the unit of the principle of pure spiritual love of Krishna. When *rati* (attachment) is mixed with *ulas* (zeal), it becomes *priti*. *Priti* creates exclusive love for Krishna and repulsion for things and persons other than Krishna and His entourage. When the idea that "Krishna is mine" is added to *priti*, it becomes *prema*. Here begins the idea that "Krishna is my own Lord and I am His servant." Add confidence to *prema* and it becomes *pranaya* wherein arises the relationship of friendship with Krishna. In *pranaya*, the idea of respect loses its hold. Add to *pranaya* the idea that "Krishna is my exclusive and dearest object of love," and it curiously turns into *mana*. Krishna, with all His greatness and power, exhibits a sort of submission to it.

With excessive melting of the heart being added, *prema* turns into *sneha*. Here ensues the relationship of a son and parents between Krishna and His devotee. In this stage, much weeping for Krishna, want of satiety in communion, and a desire to protect the interest of Krishna naturally occur. Then, an increase in desire added to *sneha* is *raga*. In this stage, a moment's separation is unbearable. Here commences the relationship of husband and wife between Krishna and His devotee. Distress attending upon want of mutual interview is happiness. *Raga*, seeing its object as new at every moment, and being itself new at every moment, converts itself into *anuraga*. In this stage, reciprocal subjection and a strong desire to accompany the lover everywhere are the principal features. *Anuraga*, infinitely rising in an astonishing state, mounting as if to madness, becomes *mahabhava*. This is inde-

scribable! From *rati* to *mahabhava*, the whole principle is
what is known as *sthayibhava*. Added to *vibhava, anubhava,
svastika*, and *sanchari*, the *sthayibhava* becomes *Krishna-
prema-rasa*, the eternal ecstasy and beatitude.

We have a perverted picture of this noble *rasa* in human life,
as life in the kingdom of Maya is a perverted reflection of spiritual life. When the soul alone works toward its proper object,
the Supreme Lord Krishna, the *rasa* is pure; when the mind
and the senses work toward a wrong object, *rasa* is degraded
and becomes deplorable. The perverted *rasa* gives us a clue as
to the nature of the noble spiritual *rasa*; hence these descriptions have been attempted in words which may also be used
to describe features of the perverted *rasa*. We ask our readers
to take care to make a definite distinction between spirit and
gross matter, otherwise a misunderstanding is inevitable.

One who studies the names, forms, attributes, and lila
of Krishna, as described in the *Srimad Bhagavatam*, with a
sincere heart, mind and strength in the company of one who
has realized the spirit, will rise higher and higher by the influence of bhakti. One who is apt to analyze everything in an
academic way can scarcely acquire the truth in matters of
spirit, as by the law of God, reason in its present state can
never reach the sphere of spirit.

In order to have the opportunity to go as far as we
have stated, one must make a further
inquiry from the heart, and the all-
beautiful Lord will then help him to
realize the spirit and rise higher and
higher in its realm. But as long as
the mind is confounded by material
allurements, there is no way to rise
beyond matter in its various forms.
The great mistake that most Western
philosophers have made is to identify the mind and the perverted ego

(*ahankara*) with the soul or spirit. This is most unfortunate.

To summarize, man in his present state has three different principles in him: (1) The *sthul* principle, or gross matter composing his body; (2) the *linga* principle, or sublimated matter appearing in the form of mind, intelligence, contaminated consciousness, and the perverted ego, by which one is bewildered within the material world. This state has been caused by the influence of maya, or the illusory energy, with the object of correcting the soul in his wrong intention to enjoy in forgetfulness of his nature as God's servant. (3) Man in fact is solely independent of Maya and her connection. The only way to get rid of the present difficulty is by the influence of pure bhakti imbibed from a true bhakta. Bhakti, as a means, elevates man up to the all-beautiful abode of Krishna, and again, as an end, maintains him with eternal *krishna-prema*.

While located in the mayik world, man must live peace-fully with the object of cultivating the spirit. In this society he must lead a pure life, avoid sins, and do as much good as he can to his fellow man. He must be humble, bearing the difficulties of life with heroism. He must not boast of any virtues or grandeur that he has, and he must treat everyone with the respect due to them. Marriage with a view toward a peaceful and virtuous life and with the intent to procreate servants of the Lord is a good institution for a Vaishnava. Spiritual cultivation is the main object of life. Do everything that helps it and abstain from doing anything which thwarts the cultivation of the spirit.

Have strong faith that only Krishna can protect you. Admit Him as your only guardian. Do everything Krishna wants you to do, and never act independent of the holy wish of Krishna. Do all that you do with humility. Always remember that you are a foreigner in this world, and be prepared to go to your own home. Do your duties and cultivate bhakti as a means to obtain the great goal of life, *krishna priti*. Employ your body, mind, and spirit in the service of the Lord. In all your actions, worship your great Lord.

Thus we have presented a summary of Sriman Mahaprabhu's life and precepts. Our gentle readers will now find that Chaitanya Mahaprabhu preached pure monotheism and chased out idolatry. He taught us that idolatry is the worship of things and persons that are not God Himself. When the sannyasis of Benares addressed Him as God Almighty, Mahaprabhu told them that it was the worst of sins to address a *jiva* as God. And He has several times denounced the worship of a form or image other than the true image of God (after which man was created). God is one without a second. "There is none to compete with Him" is the motto of Mahaprabhu's religion.

Also, Mahaprabhu showed, both in His character and preaching, the purest morality as an accompaniment of spiritual improvement. Morality, as a matter of course, will grace the character of a bhakta. If it is not seen in the character of one who presents himself as a Krishna bhakta, his sincerity may be doubted.

There are four classes of thought: atheistic, pantheistic, indifferent, and theistic. Chaitanya's religion rejects the first three as inimical to religion. He preaches pure theism alone and advises men to avoid the others.

He preaches that *Varnashram* dharma, including the caste system, is simply a social institution introduced by the *Rishis* (sages) to do good to man in society. Such social institutions should be allowed to decorate the devotees as long as they do not oppose spiritual improvement. By sending Pradyumna Misra, a rigid Brahmana, to Ramananda Raya for spiritualization, Mahaprabhu has shown that one who is aware of *Krishna-tattva* may be a guru, be he a Shudra, Brahmana, or sannyasi.

Mahaprabhu preaches the equality of men in the enjoyment of spiritual fulfillment. He preaches that human
thought should never be allowed to be shackled with sectarian
views. He preaches universal fraternity among men and
special brotherhood among Vaishnavas who are, according
to Him, the best pioneers of spiritual improvement. He
tells us that a man should earn money in a befitting way
through sincere dealings with others and should not immor-
ally obtain it. When Gopinath Pattanayaka, one of the brothers of Ramananda Raya, was being punished by the King for
immoral gains, Lord Chaitanya warned all of His associates to
be moral in their worldly dealings.

In His own early life, Mahaprabhu taught the *grihasthas*
(householders) to give all sorts of assistance to the needy
and the helpless, and has shown that it is necessary, for one
who has the power to do it, to assist in the education of the
people, especially the Brahmanas, who are expected to study
the higher subjects of human knowledge.

Sri Chaitanyadeva, as a teacher, has taught men both by
precepts and His holy life. There is scarcely a spot in His
life that may be made the subject of criticism. His taking *sannyas*, His severe treatment of junior Haridas, and other such
acts, have been viewed as objectionable by certain persons,
but we believe that those men have either been led to a hasty
conclusion or suffer from party spirit. Mahaprabhu was an
undaunted hero in the execution of his resolutions. When he
was told by some malicious Brahmanas that the emperor was
sending an army against him, he said that he wished the reign-
ing Prince would be cognizant of what he was doing. He was
amiable to everyone, yet stern in the discharge of His duty.

Once, Brahmananda Bharati, the godbrother of
Mahaprabhu's *sannyas-guru*, Keshava Bharati, appeared
before Him dressed in a tiger's skin. Mahaprabhu would not
bow down to him until he gave up the tiger skin and wore
linen cloth. He said, "The person before Me is not Bharati.

How is it that one equal to My guru could put on an animal's
skin? The sannyasis do not support the killing of beasts
for the sake of their personal use." Bharati understood that
Mahaprabhu did not like that, and he changed his apparel.
Lord Chaitanya then bowed down to him, showing proper
respect to His guru's godbrother.

Another time, Vallabha Bhatta (a scholar of great
renown) wrote what he thought to be an improved commentary on the *Srimad Bhagavatam* and showed it to
Mahaprabhu, saying that he would not submit to Sridhar
Swami. The Lord said that it was an unchaste women who
disregarded her swami (husband). This was a remark which
mortified Vallabha Bhatta and dissuaded him from express-
ing further disrespectful opinions about Sridhar Swami, the
commentator of the *Bhagavatam*.

Finally, Mahaprabhu impressed upon His disciples that
they should enter into the spirit of the *shastras* without being
confined by the words themselves. Devananda Pandit did not
understand the spirit of bhakti while reading the *Bhagavatam*,
and so he incurred offense in the course of his dealings with
the Lord's devotees. But when he captured the true spirit
of bhakti, then Lord Chaitanya embraced him and pardoned
him for all that he had done before.

The religion preached by Mahaprabhu is universal and non-
sectarian. The most learned and
the most ignorant are both entitled
to embrace it. The learned people
can accept it by studying the literatures left by the great *acharyas*.
The ignorant can have the same
privilege by simply chanting the
name of the Lord and mixing in the
company of pure Vaishnavas. The
church of kirtan invites all classes
of people, without distinction as

to caste or clan, to engage in the highest cultivation of the spirit. This church, it appears, will extend all over the world, and take the place of all sectarian institutions which exclude "outsiders" from the precincts of the mosque, church, or temple.

If you are inclined, after a study of these pages, to identify Sri Chaitanyadeva as the Supreme Lord, we would beg you not to think that God has entered into the carnal coil like the fallen men. His supreme power can bring Him down to the material world with all His glory and attributes without being touched by the lower energy of maya. To believe otherwise would be to commit the sin of minimizing His true position.

We make no objection if the reader does not believe His miracles, as miracles alone never represent the Godhead. Demons like Ravana and others have also performed miracles, which do not prove that they were God. It is unlimited *prema* and its overwhelming influence which can be seen in no one other than God Himself. In conclusion, we leave it to our readers to decide how to view Sri Chaitanya Mahaprabhu. The Vaishnavas have accepted Him as the Supreme Lord Krishna Himself. Others have regarded Him as a *bhakta-avatar* (a divine incarnation to distribute love of God). It is at the request of some Vaishnavas that we have composed the *Smarana Mangal* verses in the form of prayers for daily recitation at the time of worship. Those of you who are not prepared to accept them in that way may accept Nimai Pandit as a noble and holy teacher. That is all we want our readers to believe.

Noble readers! Pardon us for intruding on you with these pages. As servants of Sri Chaitanyadeva, it was our duty to propagate His supreme teachings and in doing a duty we are entitled to pardon for any trouble we may have given you. We are natives of Bengal and in couching our words in a foreign language we might have been liable to mistakes for which you will please forgive.

In conclusion, we beg to say that we should be glad to reply to any questions which our brethren would like to address to us on these important subjects. We feel great interest in trying to help our friends to seek the way to spiritual love.